Poems by
Nancy Jakobsson

Fold & Unfold

Design: Liz Mrofka
Cover Photography: Nancy Jakobsson
Printed by: Kindle Direct Publishing

ISBN-13: 979-8844080128

For my four directions:

Erik

Tessa   Teegan

Kris

Special thanks to my dear friend and Loveland's first Poet Laureate, Veronica Patterson, for deepening and broadening my love of poetry and for always prompting us to tell our stories, and encouraging me to write mine. And to the Writing Lab for steadfastly writing together.

"In the stir of too much motion
Hold still
Be quiet
Listen"

—Margaret Renkl, *Late Migrations*

"Every day I walk into the world to be dazzled,
then to be reflective."

—Mary Oliver

Table of Contents

Remember

Remember morning, like the first day, begins with light.
  Only those awake will see it open.
Remember to walk early when you are most
  vulnerable to beauty.
Remember winter's longest night, go inside.
  Use solitude to see.
Remember the birds, learn their songs,
  their names.
Remember each breath, a gift
  each day, practice.
Remember the trees.
  Their patience sustains me.
Remember you were conceived in grief,
  born as a promise.
Your mother's loss a small stone
  beneath her heart.
Your father, born on a small island,
  never returned.
They crossed a wide ocean to live a new story.
  Don't disappoint them.
Remember to listen in two languages.
  Remember to walk at dusk, in the perfect light.
Walk under the moon, sheltered by the stars.
  They too are your kin.

I. Walk Early

When Does Morning Come?

Is it when the black drape of night folds open,
and dark turns a soft gray, lifts like fog?
When the horizon first reveals an orange glow,
and the sun paints the mountains pink,
butters the canyon walls?
Or when the news of the day lands on my driveway
and the first garage door yawns open?
Perhaps it's when dreams break into fragments—
fade into light, and I lift the heavy blanket of sleep.
Or when I place two bare feet into the mouths of slippers
and time begins.

Nebraska Sky

In response to a watercolor by Richard Schilling

It's that kind of sky, too much sky.
So vast the horizon becomes sky.
It leaves me feeling exposed,
looking for a place to be,
a tree or boulder would do.
I didn't grow up with sky,
not this kind, bold and arrogant.
Sky was discreet, directly overhead
between buildings, houses, trees.
It had its place; it was narrow,
room for a handful of stars,
the moon when it was high.
I've come to be easy with sky,
the way it fills a day,
interrupted by mountains.

First Morning in
Sarapiqui Rain Forest

I'm in the haze of half sleep and early morning. The light is thin
and gray. The ceiling fan pushes a slow slap of air, heavy and hot.
My skin, lips, hair damp with sweat. Gradually day light cracks
through the high shutters. And it starts with a steady
hum of cicada, then suddenly in seemly orchestrated order—
the birds begin their song, they have unfamiliar names: motmots,
toucans, oropendola, kiksadee. The morning is alive with sound.
Now fully awake and opening the door. I find the
green so lush it seems to color the light. The trees drip last night's
rain. I want to say, "let there be birds. Let there be trees, giant trees
with huge leaves and flowers in abundance in pink,
red and yellow, and ferns and vines. Let there be lizards, iguanas and
frogs, and insects and bats of all kinds". Let there be the rain forest.

Lough Eske

*Italic lines are from William Butler Yeats' poem
"The Lake Isle of Innisfree."*

Grasses, trees, air, fresh with last night's
rain. The wet road absorbs my steps.

Mist hangs low in the trees,
blankets the sleeping lake,

as if night, emptied into the water,
now weeps back into the day.

On the far shore, the sun
secreted behind the clouds.

Slowly the layers lift,
settle into the trees and hills.

Sun cuts through gray
reveals the still mirrored *peace*

*slowly, dropping from the
veils of morning.*

She Had Some Mornings

She had some mornings with strange beginnings
that lasted into November.
She had some mornings with
forgetting and recycled memories.

She had some mornings.

She had some mornings full of birds,
each a new song,
some with gray clouds destined to rain,
some with drumbeats and a symphony of longing.

She had some mornings.

Some mornings had direction, east, past, west, present.
Some with purpose strayed
out open windows.

She had some mornings.

She had some mornings with
bits of dreams and broken stones,
landscapes with something left behind.

She had some far away mornings
in the shadow of high mountains,
rainforest, or lough.

Most mornings were questions.
Some lived lighter than others.
She loved mornings.

In Black and White

I.
On the side of the house
a pile of old snow
like coarse salt
peppered with dirt
is all that remains.

II.
First light reveals
a curtain of snow against
a porcelain sky, white on white
all shape and form
a skitter of tracks and
calligraphy trees
sketched on white canvas.

III.
In late afternoon
the snow begins, continues all night,
outlines trees, flowers shrubs.
Large soft flakes against
the deep black sky.
The silent work of nature
shapes the landscape in the dark.

IV.
Words track across the white page.

Where the Light Gets In

I am a student of my life,
curious about people and ideas,
stuck in wonder between past and present.

Gatherer of stones, feathers, pieces of wood.
Carrying them with me, then returning them.
I want to release things and keep stories.

In this quiet time, I wander
fallow fields and fertile valleys,
sure of few things, of that I'm certain.

Yet the light gets in.

Turn Around

How sunlight pools across the floor,
The sad, slow song of mourning doves.
The lingering scent of last night's rain.
Turn around, remember this.

How sunlight pools across the floor,
Are you waiting a for better day?
Turn around, remember this.
Before the day is fully wake.

Are you waiting for a better day?
A watching, breathing presence bring,
Before this day is fully wake.
Take it with you when you go.

A watching, breathing presence bring,
The lingering scent of last night's rain.
Take it with you when you go.
How sunlight pools across the floor.

Turn around, remember this.

To Walk Early

Remember to walk early
when you are most vulnerable to beauty.
Don't go back to sleep.
Open the door.

On summer days, leave as
the yolk of sun breaks the pink sky.
Don't miss the field of blue flax.
Bits of blue dapple the new green,
as if to fleck it with sky.

Walk along the shore.
Watch the cormorant unfold his wings,
the statue-still blue heron
stretched long on legs thin as reeds.
Or the march of tiny spotted toads
migrating into the world.

Don't miss the day,
the nesting pair of eagles fly south.
Rabbit Brush and Aspen strike gold.
A lone red duck lingers.

In the deepest days of winter,
put on your heavy coat.
Open the door, step out,
follow the tracks of rabbit and fox.
Don't go back to sleep
It's getting late.

II. Each Breath

A New Arrival

Living alone, I welcomed guests into my home.
The college friend who stayed for a week,
my son on weekends, often unannounced,
a friend dropping by, hosting dinners,
family gatherings.

> When the world shut down,
> we slid the locks on our doors
> and stayed.
> No guests allowed.
> Long quiet days,
> weeks of solitude.

Then a visit from an old friend, the counselor.
She listened to my small anxieties,
coached resilience and living into the answers.

The artist came next
with her sketchbook and paints.
We created a collage from small pieces of day.

I welcomed the Yogi, unrolling her mat.
Practiced asanas, vinyasas
and long-held shavasanas.

The poet opened her journal.
Entries and observations
grew into poems.

The spiritual teacher arrived every morning,
I greeted each of them at my door. They all stayed.

Wave of Sadness

The day after the Cameron Peak fire blew up, again, burning 20,000 acres overnight. I watched the enormous gray wall move across the foothills and mountains swallowing daylight in its path. I sent a text to a friend saying I was in "a wave of sadness." Later, she texted back, "I'm sorry you're sad". I wanted to say it's not about me. It's bigger than that, deeper. It's more like, watching the new David Attenbourough documentary "Life on Our Planet" and seeing all the loss; that in the last 50 years our wildlife population has declined by 60%, and that the polar region is warming faster than any other region on the planet. Flooded with emotion, I had to turn it off. As the fire grows larger, moves closer, is more familiar, the smoke funneled down Big Thompson Canyon, through the narrows emptying into town. Evacuated residents escaped to safety by that same route. Seven years earlier, many were chased by a wall of water. I thought about some of my favorite places, Crosier Mountain, the North Fork, Cow Creek Trail. Imagining them scorched and burned. I felt a desire to drive up and check on their well-being. Now it felt personal. How long will it take to recover, re-forest? Will I live long enough to see it? I know I'll be sad again, have waves of anxiety, followed by waves of gratitude. Or maybe like David Attenbourough, at the conclusion of the documentary, a wave of hope.

What Was Taken?

The police arrived after Midnight. The guy who lived downstairs had called 911 when he heard me scream.

Did I know the man? "No. I don't think so."
Could I describe him? "Young, dark hair, dark t-shirt, white tennis shoes."
Was I injured? "Yes, bruises on my face, neck and knuckles. Yes, I hit him."
How did he get in? "I don't know, had I locked the door, I'm not sure."
Was anything missing? "No, I don't think so."
They asked me to call if I remembered anything else.

> After, I changed the locks
> stayed with friends on the weekend,
> thought about getting a dog.
> Every dark-haired man wearing tennis shoes,
> caused fear to rise thick in my throat and chest.

I blamed myself for not locking the door.
Convinced myself it was a random act,
then changed my mind,
certain someone was trying to kill me.
I finished the school year. Moved out.
Found a new place in a different town.

I wore fear like a thick shirt
that in time it wore thin.
I reclaimed what was taken that October night.

The Last Mosquito

Yesterday while brushing my teeth.
I spied what I thought was a spider,
in the white porcelain sink,
then realized it was a mosquito.
Had it been July, not October,
and it buzzed in my ear or
poised on my arm, I would
instinctively smack it,
rendering a blood smear,
mine or some stranger's.
This malingering mosquito,
much maligned species, carrier
of Malaria, West Nile, Zika.
I could easily have sent it
on a water ride down the drain.
If it's a male it will die soon,
male life span being ten days.
Could be a female and hibernate
until Spring, laying eggs,
its offspring ready to feast
on my blood next May.

(Too late)

Booster

Here we are again, in line single file, compliantly distant. Here we are again, masked. At each check point, "Do you have any of the following, Have you been in contact with? Did you travel?" Respond negatively to all. Remember when being positive was a good thing? "Take a number—Keep your distance—Have a seat—Which arm? Just a small stick—" (Brits call it a jab). Later that night when my arm begins to ache, I wonder, am I making antibodies? How big is an antibody? Smaller than a virus? The Corona virus is 32 nanometers, What's a nanometer anyway? Picturing the image of the Corona virus, I try to imagine a spike protein stuck to a cell like a burr or thorn. This tiny invader has unraveled the world. A while back, when I was depressed about the state of the environment and we learned how some bacteria had grown resistant to antibiotics, I wrote a poem called "Revenge of the Small Things." Do all natural disasters begin small: a spark, a drop, a breeze?

Flash Mob Zorba

in Athens, not the usual coming together,
a virtual chorus, but a dance.
First, music from *Zorba the Greek*,
then a trio of young Greeks,
a man and two women,
holding hands shoulder high,
growing into a line, becoming two
lines, becoming three. Music quickens
them into a circle. Onlookers clap
the cadence. As the pace and music
reach a crescendo, the circle uncoils
into a single vibrating line of bodies
before the crowds erupts.
I find myself in tears.
The hand holding, laughing, clapping, dancing.
No masks, no social distance, no virus.

Note: The YouTube video was filmed before the 2020 Pandemic.

Inoculation

It's been more than a week and they are still in my thoughts, the couple at Walgreens. I was there for my annual flu shot, having decided to get mine early this year. I'd made an appointment for 2:30 pm. Apparently, others had the same idea, as there were six or more people sitting near the pharmacy counter, all wearing masks and socially distant. One man seemed particularly agitated and kept up a spoken stream of discontent about how long he'd been waiting and the incompetence of the staff. He was wearing baggy shorts, a faded Hawaiian shirt and a navy Vietnam Veterans cap. His wife, a white-haired Asian woman, probably Vietnamese, spoke to him in quiet tones in an attempt to settle him. His quick and loud reply was "that's because you're Asian." It was hard to interpret her look, perhaps sadly compliant. She looked down at the floor, then glanced toward me plaintively, as I was seated across from her. One or two people were called. Each disappeared behind a make-shift privacy curtain to receive an inoculation. The man's patience was long gone. "This isn't right, I've been here more than an hour." The pharmacy assistant, from behind plexiglass tried to assure him. He had difficulty hearing her, which further angered him. "This is discrimination, you don't have to be black to feel discrimination. It's because she's Asian." He was standing behind his wife, holding her large black bag in one hand. With the other he reached to touch her shoulder in a quick awkward, yet tender way. She was twisting her hands and seemed to be talking to herself. My name was called next. I walked past them, I heard. "See, she's white. This is discrimination and I won't stand for it." I wanted to look back toward her, wanted to say something, convey some understanding. Long ago, I lived with an angry man with a big voice. As I was leaving the store, I heard, "Manager, please come to the pharmacy." Later, sitting in my car, sorting through my feelings, I wondered about the man and his wife. Fifty years ago, a young Marine returned from an unpopular war with his Vietnamese wife. What did they experience, what comments, what hurts, wounds long buried? In this unbraiding time of extended stress, our fears and losses find ways to bleed out.

In Pools of Light They Wait, One by One

⌘

Winter solstice at Loveland Community Kitchen

Six feet apart, each has a story to *tell,*

of brokenness and loss, much like you and like *me.*

But their stories are rarely shared. It's more *about*

surviving this long winter night between tomorrow and *despair.*

Nowhere to go, no place to call home, like mine or like *yours.*

Grab a meal in a box and a coffee to go, a grateful nod *and*

move from the shadows into the dark, by a bridge, near the river,

places *I'll*

never know. You ask why I'm *tell-*

ing you this, on this longest night. "Why?" *you*

say. "Their lives aren't really like yours or *mine."*

A golden shovel based on Mary Oliver's line,
"Tell me about despair, yours and I'll tell you mine", from "Wild Geese."

In Time Between Time

a leaf falls but does not land
a wave crests, does not curl
a moment ago is now

thoughts form, no action taken
always is never
no need for calendars or clocks
a tick has no tock

without time
an inhale has no next
death holds no fear

in each day
a pause fills with empty
the future backs into the past

Wondering

Watching my granddaughter,
four months old.
Her world all openings and moments,
grasping, arching,
crying, smiling.
A pink bird, small yellow duck,
small fingers.
What does she name
without words?
I wonder.

Watching my friend
living her greatest fear.
Her world and time retreating,
needing, searching, wandering.
She talks of a blue watercolor,
patterns on a pillow,
shadows on the wall.
What does she know
without words?
I wonder.

III. The Patience of Trees

I Was Born

I was born on the other side of death,
sidewalks, streetlights and a tree full
of noisy sparrows.

It was the beginning or end of the
same day after a long hot summer,
city streets hop-scotching east and west.

I was born without the stars,
always looking in other windows,
when the owl appeared.

There was the waiting that crossed
the ocean of wants, and time receded
on the still hands of the old clock.

I was born across from a vacant lot.

Linden Tree

When I built my home, now more than twenty years ago,
I planted four trees, two crabapples, an Austrian Pine and a
Linden. They've all become my companions, but the Linden is my favorite.

Giver of shade. Slow to leaf-out in the Spring.
Once dressed, she wears a leafy gown
shading the east side of my house.
Fragrance giver. In July, yellow star-shaped
flowers spill a sweet, spicy fragrance, filling
the air for weeks.

Linden tea. A German friend told me of
the benefits of Linden tea, made from
flowers and seeds, better than Chamomile.
In August she releases her seeds, each
on a single wing, her gifts to the
summer wind.

She is a worthy companion during
summer storms. I sit on the front
stoop, watch the wind as it catches
her highest branches, riffles up
and down to the wind's rough blows.
She responds in exuberance.

In October her broad green canopy
turns yellow then copper. She gives up
her dress to reveal her distinctive
profile. Bare branches become bird perch,
snow catcher, moon trapper, through
the long winter until another Spring.

March

There, among the stubble and
weathered leaves
green shoots knife through
like a promise kept.
By May they'll stretch long slender blades,
like upright swords.
In June, narrow green fists will open
unfurl in flags of purple and yellow.
Planted years ago,
offspring from a friend's garden.
Every March I watch for their arrival
the return of these faithful soldiers.

The Robins Arrive

Fourteen fat robins in my Linden tree,
bright orange breasts puffed up with Spring.
They move branch to branch prospecting
with their sharp beaks.
One has a berry stolen from a neighbor's tree.
Another lands on the dogwood below,
scatters the snow plumes.
I hear their full-throated song.
They seem to settle when evening
and inevitable cold gathers,
then lift as one, fold into another tree.

July Storm

first the wind from the west.
tree branches scrape the window.
wind chimes on the patio

sound an angry response.
the Linden dips her leafy mane
from top down and up again.

thunder rolls along the mountains' wall.
a sudden clap scurries the cat.

then the rain in sheets,
the rapid staccato of hail.
the house abundant with sound,
empties the quiet.
nothing to do but listen.

then quiet slips across the sodden lawn.
a single car slows along the wet street.
the storm recedes.

Brief Encounter

While adding water to the bird bath,
I see a wasp floating on his back.
Dead, I thought.
Then he flipped over,
began to swim.
Wasps can swim?
I watched,
fascinated.
the pedaling of all six legs
frantically, rhythmically.
This small life,
precious only to himself.
He seemed to be heading toward the rim.
I felt compelled to help.
I grabbed a stick,
helped him reach safety.
He gathered himself,
without acknowledgement,
flew off.
I felt a sense of absolution,
for all my prior wasp encounters.

The Cormorant Trees

We called them The Cormorant Trees,
two old cottonwoods across the river
whose boney branches spired above the others.
One day every spring, the cormorants appeared,
a dozen or more, perching in the highest branches.
Dressed in their black overcoats,
their dark silhouettes so familiar.
One or two would strike their regal wing-drying pose.
Then one Spring, a few years back, emptiness.
The trees cut down, the cormorants gone.
I can't help but wonder—
How Mary Oliver would end this poem?

Meditation on a November Day

Steel-gray clouds wrap around the sky.
Unraked leaves fold and refold against the house.
One sparrow rocks on the wind-blown feeder.
Straggler leaves on the linden tree.
Morning paper and half-read book.
I light a fire with a single switch.

IV. Listen in Two Languages

Listen to the Silence

A Rumi cento

Your old life was a frantic running
from silence.
Your name has been erased
from the roaring volume of speech.
Learn to speak by listening,
be quiet now like the touch points
of calligraphy.
Listen to the presences
inside poems.
Few hear the hidden secrets
between voice and presence
where worlds flow.

Leave

A Tuesday or Wednesday is best—
the ends of the week have too much weight,
and it's important to travel light.
You need a starting line—
a crack in the sidewalk will do.
If a starter pistol or a whistle isn't handy
wait for the voice in your head.
Time of day can change everything.
Leaving in the dark is risky.
Leave at first light,
look around for familiar objects
a lamp post, sign, even a bucket.
A bird or cat won't work—
too unpredictable.
Pick a direction—
they're all good,
but west is the best.
If you get disoriented
make three right turns from true north.
Don't ask for directions—
everyone lies,
especially when lost.
Expect to feel bad—
it takes three days of a life time to adjust.
Avoid any sudden stops.
Movement is essential
to your original intent.
You'll know when you've arrived
by the color of the sky.

First Night in Zimbabwe

Having said our good nights, I walked to my quarters, a tiny room away from the main house and the others. Exhausted by travel I laid down on the narrow cot, planning to write in my journal. When the electricity went out, a rolling blackout, common in Bulawayo, darkness came sudden and complete, filling a space like water from the inside-out, expanding into the vastness of this place. Exhaustion turned to alertness and sleep was elusive. Enveloped by the dark, I began to listen into the night. Above me an open narrow window—I listened for outside sounds, insects or animals. I heard what sounded like singing, first female voices, then male, a rhythmical call and response, drumming soft and even, gradually louder but at a distance. The music drifted into the room and infused the dark like a mantra. It was both foreign and familiar. At some point I fell asleep. Morning came and revealed my surroundings. The strange dark night. I would not speak of it to the others.

Thembelihle

House of Good Hope Hospice for AIDs patients in Bulawayo, Zimbabwe

The air is hot and dry. Bitter smoke rises from fires cooking and
boiling bed sheets in large metal drums. Sheets and clothes wave on
lines like signal flags. Enter the white clapboard building where the
light is pale and thin, the air hot and still. Beds line both sides of
the room, everything scrubbed clean of color. Patients sleep the sleep
of the almost dead. At the far end, a young woman. She rests her
head on her hand. The sharp angles of her bones beneath thin sheets.
Her eyes large, sad and alert; her smile opens the room. "Linjani"
(I see you), I said. "Sikhona" (I am here), she replied. Lanelihle
Mthetwhadie died two weeks later.

Years pass. Still I see you.

I Didn't Do It

I didn't do it.
I thought about it.
Decided against it.
I've done it before.
That was a while ago.
This time it wasn't me.
I didn't do it.
It must have been someone else.
Someone younger and more foolish
who did it without thinking,
just rushed ahead,
no fear, just did it.
I didn't do it.
But now that I think about it,
I wish I had done it.
There's something liberating
about charging ahead fearlessly,
just doing it.
I felt that way
a long time ago—
exhilaration,
just doing it.
But this once
I'll say I did.

Namaste

The van dropped us off at Birethani about twenty miles from Pokara. We were met by six female porters, women from the village who would transport our heavy packs and staples to the lodge. Each carried a load of about eighty pounds in her straw back-carrier. They scurried ahead up the road, some in flip-flops, while we followed carrying only our day packs. The first mile of the trek followed a dirt road, then turned steeply uphill, not on a path but steps. Steps built more than 200 years ago, constructed of stone and varying in depth and width, requiring full attention, so as not to fall. I was happy to have my hiking poles. On the way we met villagers from this region called Gorum. With each encounter we exchanged Namaste. I'd come to embrace that simple greeting honoring the light or divine in each other. I half expected the cows and water-buffalo we met to bow. After about two miles the trail began to wind steeply downhill, until we reached Mala Lodge.

We were greeted by porters with glasses of chilled fruit drinks. The grounds surrounding the lodge were well maintained, lush and green, as was the valley that stretched before us, framed by foothills and low mountains. The Annapurna range in the distance was not visible, layered in late afternoon clouds. Darkness came quickly as we walked back to our rooms after dinner with our guide's promise to waken us early in the morning if the mountains were clear.

Promise Kept

A quick knock on the door at 6:00 AM followed by "the mountain is clear," repeated again and again by our guide Krista as he moved along the series of rooms. "The mountain is clear." One by one each door opened, and slowly, silently, intently the travelers stepped out, most still in their sleeping clothes, eyes fixed on the mountains, fully revealed. Their massiveness, their majesty. Giants rising above the hills and lesser mountains, taking up half the sky. As if lit from within, their brilliant whiteness seemed to illuminate the deep blue above

>Valley in shadow
>Gray-blue light of morning
>The mountain is clear.

Trip to Iceland's Blue Lagoon on a Rainy Day in October

Reykjavik recedes as we head south and enter Iceland's
rural landscape, no— moonscape. The highway
follows the coastline and the rain follows us.
The sky steel-gray and the water, a shade lighter, defined
by a thin-lined horizon and a fringe of wave at the shore.

Dark lava fields sprawl in every direction across the void.
Barrenness like no other. Black porous rock, some painted
with life-seeking moss. Miles turn into an hour and
nothing changes. Then in the distance, plumes of
steam announce the Blue Lagoon.

Tour buses spill their occupants and
a ritual begins. Showered clean, we follow
a path through cold misty air,
descend, inch by inch, into a geothermal
sea. People become floating
heads, speaking different languages.
A Babel of words rise in steam.

The lagoon, deep in a lava field
twists into narrow coves, a bridge,
a waterfall, all suspended in a gauzy gray.
Suddenly the sun cuts through to
unveil the Lagoon's name.

Geology

This particular stone
like a small gray egg
or an eye clouded by cataract
pebble of the Himalayas
once a sharp edge of mountain
washed, tumbled and smoothed
by the long wandering
Seti River.

>Rafts on the shore like three blue beached whales.
>Rapids behind and the slow slip of river ahead.
>Riverbanks wide and dry, sand, silt and nests
>of blue gray stones.
>While the guides unpack lunch from the bags
>I return to my practice of sorting and selecting,
>sorting and reselecting.
>Choosing one for another, one for another,
>a ritual to find the one to carry home.

This stone
rests with others:
black slate from a river in Norway,
granite from Mount Motopos in Zimbabwe,
another from a courtyard in Provence,
one from the Oregon Coast,
from a recent hike,
my Geology of Memories.

V. Born as a Promise

My Mother Never Forgave My Father

My mother never forgave my father
for leaving while her last grief
lay still wet behind her eyes.
His death came slow and silent
and stole her sense of self,
an absence that lasted
her long-lived life.
Her longing, like a living thing
kept like a keepsake,
in a small box,
always close at hand.

Making Soup

He's not dead yet, his parents wrote,
teaching us to know their son
three years old and dying.
He's not dead yet, I repeated
like a verse from scripture
as I placed the heavy stockpot
on the stove.

Dicing onions and garlic,
tears stream down.
Seeing his delicate profile,
small body still and perfect.
He's not dead yet, they said,
but now he is.

Slicing mushrooms in perfect half-moons,
then the celery, I pour the oil,
sauté and stir gently.
It was peaceful
in the chapel.

Hugging them, I called them precious parents.
Words I hadn't planned on saying.
When I left, a north wind blew
across the lot.
Cold for March.

Next
I added the chicken broth,
rosemary and thyme.
Quiet settled like a fog.

What She Held

Her hands were smaller than mind
soft and round.
Mine, like my dad's, were
square and angular.
I wear the wedding band
I slid from her finger on the night she died.

Hers held daughters,
mine held sons.
Hers held immigration papers,
never a college diploma.

Hers cleaned houses, her own and others'.
Hers sewed, darned, crocheted, embroidered.
Mine were better suited to a spade, a pen.
Mine planted lavender,
hers buried a daughter, husband.

She pinched pennies,
carried burdens,
held on for a long time,
held me, but never close.

Tell Me a Story

"We tell our stories to live." —*Joan Didion*

1.
Tell me a story, Ama.
Make it about a little girl
who lives in a house in a forest
with all the forest animals,
and she has a kitten and a puppy.
The puppy gets lost.
And can the girl also become a mermaid?

2.
Tell me your story of loss.
Tell me who died, when, what happened.
Tell me how your life has changed.
And who are you now?

3.
Tell a story that's never been told
to the Raven. The Raven will hold it,
care for it, bring it to an open field.
When it has wings, set it free.
It will return to the Story Teller
as a butterfly.

4.
Tell me a story, Ama.

Death's Weight

I.

I remember when we put down our dog.
The setter-lab who grew with my sons.
Who ran miles in the fields behind our house,
ran behind the car when we left for town,
chased the school bus, the wind.
Now he lay on the cold steel table.
The vet promised it wouldn't take long,
Then slid the needle into his skinny leg.
I wanted to tell him the truth, to say good bye,
Nestle my head next to his, breathe into his fur.
All I could say was, "You're a good boy."
I felt it—the weight of death.

II.

I had felt it before, that weight,
on the night my mother died.
Alone with her body,
I removed her wedding band, her watch,
lifted her arm heavy with death,
like a bag of sand or soft earth.
The inertness so actual.
Life absent as a stone.
I left with what I could carry,
leaving the rest.

III.

Once on a hospice visit, I carried a body.
A woman's daughter wanted her mother
to die in bed, but we moved her
from the chair where she had died.
Lifting, I caught my breath, surprised
by the effort it took.
Then we dressed her
in a white cotton gown,
raised her head, each arm,
to slide it down her bony frame.

IV.

I left knowing what the daughter would carry.

Broken Home

After the relentless wind blows
half the day and through the night,
all is still. The sky is clear.

Beneath the crabapple tree
is the birdhouse I bought at the craft fair
from a man who said he made
the houses for therapy. On its side
the roof is broken into slender pieces
scattered beneath the tree.

> I remember another house blown apart
> by February winds,
> a forever house, under construction.
> In morning's first light, silver sheets
> of insulation scattered in the field,
> shards of window glass, siding, 2x4s,
> a chaos of brokenness.
> The frame leaning to one side.
>
> The house got built, the family moved in.
> Then, like the house, the marriage broke apart.
> Forever lasted five years.
> In my dreams the house is never straight
> The walls can't hold the anger.
> There are rooms no one enters.

I place the broken birdhouse against
the trunk of the crabapple tree,
prop the pieces of roof back into place.
I wonder if the man still builds them for therapy.
I'll buy another in the Spring.

The Canyon Narrows

We're on our way to Rocky Mountain National Park, my grand-daughter and I. She is in back in her booster seat. She will start first grade next week and this is our final outing of the summer. I have wanted to take her to the Park since I volunteered two years ago, but she has not wanted to go. Today she seems to be ready. She wants to know how long it will take, what animals we will see, could she maybe buy a stuffy and could we stop for a waffle cone. When we pass the Dam Store, she asks about the large water pipe over the highway. Soon we're in the canyon narrows. Her questions stop. She's quiet and then says, "Ama, I'm scared." "Why?" I ask. "Because the mountains go straight up, the river is way down there and the road is narrow." I assure her I will drive safely and suggest she look for bighorn sheep. I watch her through the rearview mirror. She's looking out the window, her face serious with intent.

We are both quiet until we pass the Cherry Cider store and I say, "Perhaps we can stop there on our way home. Then she says, "You know, sometimes I like being scared." "Tell me about that," I say. "It's the kind of scared when your heart is beating fast and you feel excited, but you don't think anything bad is going to happen." I reply, "I know what you mean. Sometimes, I like that feeling too." She quickly responds, "You do?"

Neither of us says anything for a good long time.

Seeds of Grief

A child laid in a hospital bed.
A headache became a brain tumor.
The mother came every day,
the father worked.
They sat together every evening.
They waited.
Time passed.
The child died.
Their only child.
She, inconsolable.
He shut down.
She broke down, they broke apart.
Time passed.
They came together,
clung to each other and hope.
Time passed.
A seed of grief found fertile ground.
Late the next summer I was born.

Unpacking the Past

Lift and unsnap the large green lid,
release the smell of old wool and time.
On top, a woven table runner in colors of earth and fire,
my grandmother's, whom I never knew.
Next, in its official triangle shape,
the flag handed to my mother
more than sixty years ago.
There's a crib blanket embroidered
in tiny perfect stiches.
Was it mine or Margaret's?
Lifting each piece gently, remembering,
I unfold the past.
On the bottom, I reach my goal—
a coffee service, platter, trays,
tarnished black by decades of un-use.
I spend hours polishing, releasing memories,
surprised by what lasts,
the stubbornness of things both soft and hard,
knowing tomorrow I'll pack it all again,
until another time.

VI. Walk at Dusk

This Is a Prayer

For my aging cat and
her sagging belly.

For the neighbor's old dog
left outside in the cold.

For the birdhouse blown down,
shattered pieces on the ground.

For the single sparrow
on the feeder's narrow ledge.

For our country,
its divisions' sharp edges.

For the earth's warming crust
rising seas, diminishing forests.

For Jim's chemo
       Cathy's radiation
              Jim's ablation
                     Gail's medications.

For grace,
       for grace
              for amazing grace.

For the bees.

There Is a Field

Honoring Rumi

I'll meet you there or
on the path that leads around
the still dark pond at dawn.
I'll meet you on the trail,
in the shadow of Hallett's Peak as
Aspen gold dips deep in Emerald Lake.

Come sit with me and wait
for the speechless full moon.
I'll meet you at the coffee shop
beneath the ancient elm.
I will listen as you
read a favorite poem.
The world is too full to talk about.

In Remembrance

We gather around the table in your dining room; you are not there.
But of course you are, under the words, slightly below the laughter.
We eat pizza and drink wine, served in your glasses, less one. We
hold you in our collective breath, waiting. This is the night your
husband would share what would be his most generous gift to us, in
a small oval jar. We wait to receive a ceremony, sweet and awkward,
"in remembrance." I glance at your photograph on the wall, remem-
bering it from your memorial. What would you have made of all of
this? The last time I was in this room, you lay in a hospital bed in a
cloud of blue very still. I left that day knowing it would be my final
visit. Yes, this is your dying room. How like dining room, your
dying room.

I Only Met Him Once

I only met him once. Twice if you count the time at the coffee shop. When I asked John about Matt, he hadn't seen him in days. "Maybe in the morgue, jail or detox." He kind of laughed, but it wasn't a joke. I'd driven them to the dentist office, John riding shotgun, Matt in the back seat. Looking straight ahead, conversation came easily. John talked about past jobs, current troubles, moving forward, going to the dentist. He told me he and Matt were alcoholics, but were glad they didn't use meth. He said, "It messes up your body, especially your teeth." He asked me to pull over so he could retrieve a ball in the street and toss it back over the schoolyard fence. Two weeks later I got a call, then a text with a photo. "Yes, that's John." He'd been with Matt. Drunk, then blacked out, then dead. The coroner hasn't released his report. Would anyone write an obituary? He was 31. His name was John. I only met him once.

I Want to Dream

I want to dream what water dreams,
sleep the sleep of trees,
hum an autumn day,
shout the eagle's flight.

I want to whisper a smooth stone,
dance a yellow moon,
sing a dark cloud.
And when sorrow takes my breath away,
I want to be the wind.

Out of the Cold

We open the doors early.
A hand full of people step out of the cold into the light,
stomping off snow and the night,
as they head to a table or booth.
I work the drink cart: coffee, tea, hot chocolate, juice,
navigating the cart between the tables.

Joe asks for coffee, four sugars and grape juice.
As he tugs off his thick wool cap,
he tells me he slept in the cemetery last night,
how the zipper on his sleeping bag broke,
how his steel-toed boots cause frostbite.
Then goes back to reading yesterday's paper.

R. takes coffee, two creamers and a hot chocolate pack.
In her thick voice, she opens most conversations with
"You know, I'm a college graduate."
She looks to be in her sixties.
She has a plastic neck brace and
uses a three-toed cane.
She's waiting to have back surgery
but needs to have a place to recover.
She never leaves without saying,
"God bless you people."

The young woman in an oversized parka,
short reddish hair, attractive, and an athletic build
takes the back booth. She likes herbal tea
and brings her own mug. She used to carry her stuff
in a box and two plastic bags.
Always sits alone, stays until we close up breakfast.
Today she's empty-handed, no bags.
 I don't ask but I wonder if she's found a place to stay.

9:00 dishes washed and tables wiped down.
I take off my mask, plastic apron and gloves.

Head home.

To Hear

I want to hear a baby's first cry
an old man's last breath,

thunder echo from the canyon wall,
the whoosh of wild geese wings.

I want to hear sounds of a city street at dawn,
my father's voice forgotten in childhood.

I want to hear the silence beneath the heart.
blood pulse through my smallest vein.

the cottonwoods sigh after long days of drought,
a dragonfly closing his wings.

I want to stop the squeal of tires before the crash,
the click of a bullet entering a chamber.

I want noise to rest so I can
hear stones sing in the river's bed.

Sometimes It Takes the Dreamer
a Long Time to Notice

In my dream, I am given a white shell-
like sphere, almost translucent,
like fine porcelain, thin as an egg shell.
Holding it, I can feel a slight vibration.
There's a hole large enough to see through.
Looking inside I see a kaleidoscope of blue,
tiny butterflies in shades of blue,
wings tips fringed in white.
moving in precise patterns, occasionally
settling in one unified motion,
as if choreographed.
A wonder of aliveness. I wake
feeling both joy and sadness,
I received this fragile gift. What
is mine to do?